The Calendar's Whim

Selected works by Margaret Randall

Poems:
Wild Card
This Honest Land
Home
Time's Language II: Selected Poems 2019-2023
Time's Language: Selected Poems 1959-2018
Vertigo of Risk
Stormclouds Like Unkept Promises
Out of Violence into Poetry
Starfish on a Beach: The Pandemic Poems
As If the Empty Chair / Como si la silla vacía
The Rhizome as a Field of Broken Bones
About Little Charlie Lindbergh

Nonfiction:
Pages Lost and New
More Letters from the Edge
Letters from the Edge
Last Words
Artists in My Life
Thinking About Thinking
I Never Left Home: Poet, Feminist, Revolutionary
Che on My Mind
Haydée Santamaría: She Led by Transgression
Exporting Revolution: Cuba's Global Solidarity

Praise for Margaret Randall and *The Calendar's Whim*

"For as long as I've had the distinct pleasure of knowing Margaret Randall and her work, neither she nor her work have ever shied from the penetrating questions. Questions that simultaneously invite hope and devastation. Questions like, instead of the urge to erase our most insufferable histories, what if we simply lived 'a history we can be proud to tell children and grandchildren'? She's proving to be timeless. Her poems in this collection, however, continue to age with the times, 'growing with power as they do.'"

— **Hakim Bellamy,** inaugural City of Albuquerque Poet Laureate and author of *Commissions y Corridos*

"As introduction to this magnificent collection written in her ninth decade, poet Margaret Randall interviews herself. *The poet in me speaks to the world, and I am part of the world*, says Randall, where writing is her way of harvesting and dispersing fruits of memory and knowledge. She explores the liminal spaces of existence, possible when less busy, with slow curiosity. Vast themes ignite these poems: colonization, racism, lesbian love, resistance, art, climate catastrophe, family, aging and community. This is a book suffused with curiosity and wisdom, and bears witness to past and current times of struggle and resistance. We are exhorted to 'own the trouble / subvert and defeat it / to save yourself and memory.' This poet does not back down. Instead, her vast body of powerful work drowns out 'that bully chorus / meant to erase us / from our lives.'"

— **Tina Carlson,** author of *A Guide to Tongue Tie Surgery*

"Approaching age ninety, Margaret Randall remains very much a poet of now, not in spite but because of her long and distinguished history. That is to say, our contemporary moment has circled back around to the concerns that have long animated her work.... Her fearlessness is by no means limited to ideological struggle, however, and among the most affecting poems in *The Calendar's Whim* are those confronting the fear of death that looms at her age, a subject she approaches with the same refusal of shame and self-pity that characterizes her earlier writings on sexual assault and incest. As she has always protested, she is not a 'political poet'; she refuses that level of compartmentalization in favor of presenting the whole package of human experience. Life itself is her subject."

— **Garrett Caples,** author of *Lovers of Today*

"Celebrated poet and activist Margaret Randall assumes her role as sage and seer to remind us of the deep-rooted power of chronicle in our struggle for a more human world. Her poems sing their truth, challenging us to 'call on memory and start fighting back.' Indeed, these pages are a resounding testament to the sway of poetry—nearer to truth than history."

— **Katherine M. Hedeen,** translator of Antonio Gamoneda's ***Burn the Losses***

The Calendar's Whim
poems

Margaret Randall

Casa Urraca Press
ABIQUIÚ

Copyright © 2026 by Margaret Randall

All rights reserved.

Thank you for supporting authors and artists by buying an authorized edition of this book and respecting all U.S. and other relevant copyright laws by not reproducing, scanning, or distributing any part of it in any form without express written permission from the publisher, except as permitted by fair use. You are empowering artists to keep creating, and Casa Urraca Press to keep publishing, books for readers like you who actually look at copyright pages.

This work of poetry contains references to real people and events. Some historical details may have been changed for privacy reasons and for creative license.

This book and its components are human-authored and human-designed without the use of artificial intelligence. No part of this work may be used to train AI technologies or develop machine learning language models, or for similar purposes, without the express written permission of the publisher.

Cover photograph by Barbara Byers.
Author photograph by Gay Block.
Set in Nobel and Odile.

"As If Dreaming" first appeared in a special edition of fifty copies as a postcard from Longhouse Press, West Brattleboro, Vermont.

29 28 27 26   1 2 3 4 5 6 7

First edition

ISBN: 978-1-956375-48-0
Library of Congress Control Number: 2026930659

CASA URRACA PRESS

an imprint of Casa Urraca, Ltd.
casaurracapress.com

For my children,
Gregory, Sarah, Ximena and Ana;
for my grandchildren,
Lía Margarita, Martín, Daniel, Ricardo Sergio, Sebastián,
Juan, Luis Rodrigo, Mariana, Eli, and Tolo;
for my great-grandchildren, Guillermo, Emma Nahuí,
Julia, Lucas, Mehdi;
and for all those born after I am gone:
branches of my tree.

Contents

3	Margaret Randall interviews Margaret Randall
13	Twenty Poems of Despair and a Song of Hope
20	Double Exposure
21	I Changed the Story
22	Beauty Kills
24	All That Glitters
26	The Anniversaries
28	Your Inheritance
30	The Camera
32	Safe Passage
34	Matching Temperatures
35	One of the Lucky Ones
37	Refugee
39	Keep Out
42	National Pastime
43	With Flowers and Sympathy
45	Querencia
46	1984
47	If I Told You
49	Out of an Ochre Haze
51	Right Where You Hid It to Keep It Safe
52	Patience in the Eye of the Storm
53	Heirloom Seeds
54	Best Friend and Alter Ego
57	Witness
59	Roberta Flack (1937-2025)
60	There Will Be Room for Breath
62	We Hold Hands
65	What Is Life
66	A Periodic Table of Personal Elements
68	Understanding I Don't Understand

70	Facts
73	A Know-It-All Conceit
75	They Think They Know
77	Every Step Forward Brings Ghostly Images
79	Own the Trouble
80	The Day Before
81	My Voice
83	Lies
85	The Genius of Lime
86	The Integrity of Fire
88	Adding a Piece to the Puzzle
89	An Arrow Hit Its Mark
91	Transitions
94	Christmas 2024
96	A Garden of Possibility
98	Their Up, My Down
100	The Lake
101	Maren
104	"What I Have Done No One Has Done Before"
106	We Whisper Before We Speak
108	What We Already Know
111	The Porter
115	Your Story
117	Theater of Folly
118	Your Contribution
119	We Are We
121	Nothing for Tomorrow
123	Tomorrow
124	The Butcher's Dishonest Thumb
125	Definition
126	Swimming in Defeat
127	Smoke Signals

130	When the Countdown Begins
132	No Thank You
134	Mother's Day
136	Listen to the Silence
137	Free from Monetary Exchange
139	Poems Must Say Something
141	The Prompt
142	Protected Speech
144	Surf
145	Ferocious Tenderness
147	Dependent on the Calendar's Whim
150	The Book Remains
152	The Freedom They Find So Confusing
155	The Sun Below Our Feet
156	She Began to Speak
157	As If Dreaming
158	The Archive
160	Where Do We Look
162	Where I Am Going
165	*About the author*

"We've come up against the church, Sancho."
—*Miguel de Cervantes*

"We often talk about systemic violence
as something abstract, institutional.
But what if it's closer to muscle memory?"
— *Damien Davis*

Margaret Randall interviews Margaret Randall

Why do you want to do this interview? Isn't it an ostentatious way of "talking to yourself," an exercise in narcissism?

Perhaps. But the poet in me speaks to the world and I am part of the world.

Are there things you can only ask yourself?

I can ask anyone, but I might be the only one who answers. It's like peeling an orange; some of the white pith between skin and flesh inevitably remains. That's where the secrets live.

You seem obsessed with secrets.

I am obsessed with the damage they can do. Those secrets families keep, which so often send children on lifelong quests for what really happened, why they suffer from anxiety or even PTSD. Those kinds of secrets are anathema to truth, to growth. What remains when what we know as truth has been stripped away and replaced with lies that protect the guilty. In a time when official policy subverts truth in every voice, and memory is tarnished by deliberate cruelty, I look for transparency everywhere.

Transparency may be another one of your obsessions...

I question your use of the word "obsession," but yes, I am viscerally annoyed by subterfuge, by formalistic phrases meant to console but which only lie. "Everything's going to be alright" is at the top of the list, when you've revealed a serious illness or some other situation that may be life-threatening or fatal. Even seemingly harmless exchanges like "How are you? Fine, thank you," when reality is otherwise. I am careful to choose words that reflect reality, that honor meaning.

Come on! Those are harmless phrases that only reflect people's good intentions, their desire to make the person they're speaking to feel better.

I prefer honesty, a true honoring of memory.

Have you always had this interest in memory?

No, and I haven't always been able to access my own memory, personal or collective. When I was younger, only my now felt real. In broken societies, we are trained to be self-absorbed. Straight white men, because their earliest education is rooted in entitlement, come by this most easily. If you are female or identify as any one of the other genders, if you are queer or dark-skinned or poor, you may not recognize a self in which you can be absorbed. If you're lucky and courageous enough, you learn to construct yourself. Age brings the fortune of memory. Very old age sears memory into your spine and it grows branches, sprouts leaves, may even cover itself in budding fruit. Then the trick is to disperse that fruit before it falls into the abyss or rots in place.

Are you talking about philanthropy?

I don't understand the word.

Are you talking about art?

I don't believe in talking about art. Art is art. It speaks for itself.

But you have written pages, spoken volumes, about art.

My bad.

Come on now, don't be cute.

Nothing stops me more quickly than that word: cute. Okay, I'll try saying it another way. As a poet, I've learned that the surest way to a bad poem is talking around your subject, creeping up to the edge but never taking the leap. I don't want to describe. I want to transcend description, transmit experience in a way that puts the reader or listener right there, out in the cold or consumed by its heat.

At your age, have you been able to assimilate the broad range of identities expressed today, the variety of pronouns, including "they," which I imagine carries with it a grammatical problem for someone so concerned with linguistic fidelity?

I admit that it's not always easy for me to switch one pronoun for another with someone I've known for years. Sometimes I must remind myself to use the correct one, to demonstrate respect for that person's choice. Still, it's worth the effort. More importantly, I've never really believed there are only two genders. All we need do is look around us to understand that a binary world is stereotypical, absurd. And I don't believe our list of pronouns is anywhere near complete. It's clear to me that there are as many different identities as there are humans. Individuality is, after all, our most authentic trait.

You are a woman who has had a number of long-term relationships with men and given birth to four children. Yet for the past almost forty years you've lived with a woman, and you call yourself a lesbian. How did you come to that identify? Did it respond to a better understanding of who you are—perhaps always have been—or was it an expedient choice?

I've been honest about my identity as I've grown to understand it. I came up with the assumption that falling in love with a man was my only option. And I did fall in love, and some of those relationships gave me children who are central to my life. In retrospect, though, I don't believe that what I knew with those men was love, at least not as I am able to define it today. But there are good memories as well as painful ones. I was close to fifty years old when the social and cultural circumstances in which I was living opened me to the possibility of loving a woman. And I jumped at that possibility, fully and without hesitation. I began calling myself a lesbian not because I needed a label for myself but because it was an important political statement at the time. I identify as a lesbian, but to be entirely honest I should say that I would love Barbara whatever her gender.

And your most authentic experiences?

Becoming a mother four times over, becoming a mother each of those four times and simultaneously all of them together. Gregory. Sarah. Ximena. Ana. Giving life to my son and each of my three daughters, learning to know their unique selves, their diversity, character, and beauty as I watch them grow and move out into their own worlds. Witnessing my children give birth to their children, my grandchildren to my great-grandchildren, and feeling myself a part of that unbroken lifeline, that creative force. Loving a woman, Barbara, who loves me in equal measure, each supporting the other's wholeness without reserve. Learning trust moment by material moment. Inhabiting or touching other cultures, places, peoples, times. Knowing terror and pushing through it to speak my convictions. Having lived long enough to be able to speak those convictions fearlessly. (I almost said "no matter the price," but that's not true because I understand, finally, that there may be some prices I am unable to suffer.) Rejecting all religions and other authoritarian institutions and their dogmas, understanding the terrible damage they do. Visiting ancient ruins, immersing myself in their social climates and conversing with their ghosts. Standing still in places so wondrous they might be dreams. Reveling in imagination...

Stop! You might as well be reciting a laundry list, "the seventy thousand wonders of the world."

You asked. The world is beautiful, pulsing with life, with discovery, with creativity. And its destruction is one of the horrors we endure today.

So, let's talk about the horrors we are enduring.

The Trump administration and other supernationalist takeovers around the world. Call them by their names. Here in my own country, a situation I couldn't have imagined in terms of its disregard for humanity, penchant for destruction, and utter cruelty. The candidate made his intentions clear, but not enough of us listened. Then the president unleashed his disdain for anyone but a coterie of bombastic, frightened, obsequiously loyal billionaire friends. We are startled by the rapidity with which he's rolled out his punitive agenda. We are living in a time unlike any we've experienced up close and personal— reminiscent of Nazism's persecution of Jews and others who were "different," the U.S. bombing of Hiroshima and Nagasaki, Latin America's dirty wars with their massive disappearance campaigns, the U.S. war in Vietnam, the Killing Fields of Cambodia, Israel's genocide in Palestine. The list goes on. And we've been forced to sit back and watch as this modern-day dictator replaces anyone in a position of power who threatens to oppose him, then implements one policy after another aimed at erasing our hard-won freedoms, robbing us of future.

What can we do?

That's the question. An estimated twelve million of us took to the streets in a first concerted act of resistance, an encouraging showing. And the demonstrations have continued, bigger and louder and aimed at more specific goals. But I'm having trouble connecting this display of resistance with its impact on a rogue administration. We tend to think of cause and effect rationally, a mistake when dealing with a sociopathic mind. As we experienced this assault, we heard reassurances, people who pointed to the Constitution or the courts as safeguards against the disintegration of a "democratic society." We've seen how fragile those safeguards are, how quickly they've eroded. Perhaps we finally understand why "the good Germans" couldn't prevent the Holocaust. What I'm feeling right now is that all we can do is speak up, do what we can to defend the most vulnerable among us, and continue to create: whatever it is that each of us makes or does. My hope is that viable strategies will reveal themselves. But hope itself is fleeing my vocabulary.

You identify first and foremost as an artist. And you have often said that you reject the label "political poet," that you don't even acknowledge such a thing as a "political poem." Yet you seem eager to talk about our current political situation.

I don't call myself a political poet because I write about anything and everything. And I believe all subjects are fair game for poetry. A poem, no matter its theme, is good if it works, bad if it doesn't. You can call the times we live in political, but I prefer to call them human. Increasingly, the old labels are losing their usefulness. Among Republicans we hear an occasional call for reason. And the Democratic Party, in its arrogant ineptitude, allowed this onslaught of fascism. Throughout my adult life, I've been involved with several revolutionary movements led by parties or organizations that claimed they were fighting for equality. I have lost beloved comrades to their excesses. I have seen those movements' shortcomings as well and have been profoundly disappointed when people I believed in showed themselves to be biased or corrupt. Today I would say that I have lost my belief in top-down political organization. And partisan politics are too narrow a measure of these times. Isms have lost their relevance. Immigrant families are being torn apart whether they identify with "red" or "blue" values. Poverty, abandonment, hunger, exile attack us irrespective of party affiliation. This isn't politics, it's life.

Let's talk about voice. You've spoken a great deal about your journey finding and honing your own voice. Lately, though, you've engaged other voices in your work. Three recent books—*Letters from the Edge: Outrider Conversations*, *More Letters from the Edge*, and *Letters that Breathe Fire*—all have as their materia prima the voices of others, in the form of letters written to you throughout your life. What value do you see in using those voices in your work?

The value of community. The value of looking at specific times and places and events from multiple, diverse, sometimes contrary angles. I first understood the importance of listening to other voices many years ago when I was engaged in oral history projects, most often with women in Latin America. Not only the stories they told, but how they told them. The secrets they exposed. The desires they laid bare. The cultural differences. Or maybe it was earlier still, when as a very young woman living in New York City I sought the advice of the playwright Paddy Chayefsky and he suggested I stand on a streetcorner in Times Square and listen to bits of conversation, memorize accents, explore the rhythms of communication. Form and content. The phrases I heard entered my poetry. They hooked me on language itself. These much more recent books, based on long-term correspondence, take this exploration further. Because of the tension between the letters themselves, which are distant in time, and my commentary on them, which is current, I venture to say they constitute a new genre, a way of looking at history that is immediate and intimate even as it opens windows on important historic periods. But my voice isn't absent from these books. It is the connective tissue that gives perspective to them.

Given the grave political picture that you painted just a moment ago, how do you garner the energy for so much writing, so many books? How do you keep from feeling paralyzed, immobilized?

It's what I know, as natural by now as breathing, how I keep on living. And in my old age I have the privilege of time. I've developed a discipline that enables me to give full rein to my creativity. I start working at three or four in the morning; it's my priority every day.

It sounds as if you believe you have all the answers, that age has endowed you with some sort of wisdom.

No. There are few things I distrust more than the self-styled guru who makes a business of supposed wisdom in our commodity-oriented societies. If age has taught me anything, it's that what I don't know far outweighs what I do. There are always more questions than answers. We think we understand an issue only to discover that our knowledge is partial at best. At this point, what I'm left with is curiosity. Tolerance for other viewpoints if they're not arbitrary, unkind, based in superstition, or exclusionary. I say my piece and continue to listen for those other voices in our powerful chorus.

Twenty Poems of Despair and a Song of Hope

*Reversing Pablo Neruda's
sequence to fit our time.*

1.
That story about a rib
built devious cages
and millennia of battered women.
We are still searching
for escape routes
as we smile and lower our eyes.

2.
From quarks and leptons
to the vastness of our universe
and back,
we dissect the parts
but forget the soil,
water and air
of our suffering home.

3.
Horse, gun and cross
brought deception to the lake
where Moctezuma reigned
and a small woman
known as La Malinche
translated the language
of conquest in impossible time.

4.
To the north
of that disappearing lake
native peoples
lived communally,
then Europe
brought crude ownership
and centuries wronged
by stolen land, whiskey,
and the disease of progress.

5.
White violence
descended on Africa,
raping villages,
kidnapping human beings
and forcing them
body to body
onto overcrowded ships
sailing to a hostile land,
then auctioned them off
according to strength
and durability:
slavery's cruel legacy.

Ghostly hoods and
flaming crosses,
strange fruit
hanging from innocent trees,
the ominous whistle
in the night.

6.
German cattle cars
sewed a landscape with fear,
leaving heaps
of skeletal bodies
—some still alive—
piles of gold teeth,
human hair,
unchosen tattoos,
sending survivors
looking for a safe home
even if it meant
erasing others
from their land.

7.
In a blinding explosion
"Little Boy" delivered death
among the cherry blossoms.
Bodies near the epicenter
evaporated in scorched air
leaving only the shimmering
silhouettes of their lives.
Faces patched many times over
answer with a rare beauty.
Then we did it again.

8.
Ho Chi Minh's trail
scattered tenacious seeds
in tunnels beneath
the invaders' feet,
coaxed victory on bicycles
until David's slingshot
launched the stone
that pierced Goliath's brow.

9.
Rwandan fields ran red
with the blood
of sisters and brothers,
husbands and wives.
When Hutus murdered Tutsis
they sometimes traded houses
at night.
The world looked away.

10.
When it was Serbia
and Croatia's turn
the victims were white
and the world took notice.

11.
Palestinians resist
the bulldozers
turning their homes
to rubble,
carry mattresses
and cooking pots
into caves as they scream
unanswered questions
at encroaching settlers.

Bombs strip teachers
from schools,
doctors from hospitals,
erase children
through decades of atrocity
by a country
that wants the world
to believe it is the victim:
genocide masked
as religious prophecy.

12.
In Ireland they called them
The Troubles,
quiet name for a war
like so many,
that claimed religion as its source.
Dirty blankets
and end-to-end hunger strikes
wove chains of human resistance.

13.
South America's Dirty Wars
left holograms of disappeared:
the absent hand on a shoulder,
silenced voice,
lonely bench in the park,
broken memory
where lost generations
should be giving birth
to children of their own.

14.
Stonewall described
the way out
of our shadowy closets of shame,
gave us a rainbow land
on which to stand and speak.

15.
Bodies rebel
when their assignment
at birth is wrong.
We must honor their journey
as we would honor
the integrity of a towering oak
or delicate trickle of water
deep at the back of a cave.

16.
In this twisted tradition of horror,
he told us what he would do.
No surprise
to those who listened.

17.
Now this is no longer
our land
from sea to shining sea.
Our gardens go to rot.
Every day another flower dies.

18.
Do not obey
the heartless imposter
who trembles at the sound
of our voices,
cowers before the power
of our art.

19.
Our resistance
cuts him to size,
makes space for us
to breathe and fight.

20.
Only when millions rebel
in righteous disobedience
will we be able
to send him away for good.

21.
No room for his hate
in a nation diverse
and welcoming to all.

Double Exposure

The image that tripped
this morning's escape
from the dream
where I battled direction
and lost,
steadies me
as I move into day.

The word that fell
on its head,
leaving a trail of blood
from fairytale
to history book,
burns the palms
of my arthritic hands.

I am the woman
who shuffles
behind her walker
breathing the rarified air
of discovery,
reinventing a new language
to tell an ageless story.

I appear in the picture:
an advertisement for spring
superimposed
on winter's early grave.
I am wearing a smile
that banishes every secret
as it reflects the avalanche of now.

I Changed the Story

I changed the story
so those who listened
might imagine
their own son or daughter.

One child's death
from starvation
is cruelty
all hearts understand.

Thirty thousand dead children
is a statistic like so many
that appear in headlines
soon forgotten.

I changed the story.
Will you listen now?

Beauty Kills

> *"If you control the narrative,*
> *you control the memory.*
> *If you control the memory,*
> *you control the future."*
>
> —Damien Davis

Erase the open wounds
time hasn't healed
because we keep poking them
with fingers of hate.

Censor them from classrooms
to protect the feelings
of those poor innocents
who shouldn't have to be ashamed
of their white skin.

Keep that ugliness
from tender ears.
A whisper of reality
can do a world of harm.

Present the crimes
as beautiful
as long as committed
against those
we only read about
but do not know.

If beautiful and grand,
it writes a history
we can be proud to tell
to children and grandchildren.

They, like we, will ignore
the stories buried
beneath all that fictitious beauty:
our national monuments
to death.

All That Glitters

The pot at the end of the rainbow
holds fools' gold,
dull coins not even the oarsman
on the River Styx
would place in a dead man's eyes.

Do not blame yourself
for believing the fairytales,
lies that lulled you to sleep
night after night
from before your birth.

To battle their secrets,
you must sacrifice your heart
to wildness,
spit out the lies
stuck to the roof of your mouth
like cotton candy at the fair.

All that glitters, every message
that briefly lights the sky
as it screams: *you need me*
or *I will keep you safe*
was written to break your wings.

Remove the rose-colored glasses
they sent you as a bonus.
I will wait, but not too long,
while you hone the courage
to call memory back
from where she trembles in fear.

Wrap yourself in her temperature
and use your power
to change the script.

The Anniversaries

What do they mean, these anniversaries
laboring up my steep trail of memories
or coming for me at the speed of light?

Eighty years since the end of a war
that promised to be the last.
Blackouts and Bundles for Britain
long ago replaced by pictures
of those camps,
now memorials to death,
unwanted numbers
beneath sleeves pulled down
to cover stories impossible to tell.

Fifty since Saigon's U.S. embassy roof
shook with the defeated
clamoring to get out alive.
I still call it Ho Chi Minh City
remembering the simple man
who called upon a nation's dignity.

Fifty as well since Roque succumbed
to his murderer's siege of torture
and died somewhere
in that small country
he loved with his life.
He will never be older than 39
but his poems age,
growing in power as they do.

And Miguel, who went down
in a blaze of gunfire
on a Chilean street:
his final moment also claims
the half century mark.
So many to mourn as they parade
before my tired eyes.

Why do these dates pierce my heart
when the in-between days
pass unobserved, minor milestones
that fail to sound fierce drumbeats
in my ears?

They are the pictures framed in time,
the places I visit
when living memory crumbles
along its edges
threatening to leave me stranded
on islands of forgetting.

I light a secular candle
and write my gratitude
on the calendar I've carried
through this long life
for each of the names
that spell community,
reminding me I belong.

Your Inheritance

Your fine inheritance
glows in the dark:
chance or obligation.
You toss it
from hand to hand
afraid it will
burn your flesh.

Beware the oversize
mango pit,
devour as much
of the succulent fruit
as you can:
its juices running
between your teeth,
its sweetness measured
against the rigors of duty.

What of the secrets?
What of the lion
that won't be tamed,
pain nestled
between your ribs,
shadows that linger
behind curtains of night?

That fork in the road
is always just
a few feet ahead.
You can choose to go right,
left, or stop.
But know if you stop
it may become
your final resting place.

The Camera

He looked up
and posterity held his gaze
beneath the black beret
with its single star.
His dream left the crowd
behind.
He couldn't have known
the image would plant
eternity between his ribs.

Avoiding the penetrating stare
of the large man at her side,
a six-year-old girl
looks down at her tensed hands
trying to hide
from a shadow of silence
she wouldn't understand
for half her life.

A face in a crowd helped
solve a murder
thirty years after
an unknowing photographer
snapped the shutter.
That barely visible meeting of eyes
reveals another tale
of fear and circumstance.

Believe the instant
that speaks mechanical certainty
of light and shadow
we of poor eyesight
call black and white.

The camera itself is only
optic precision,
finely-ground glass
and steel hinges
obeying a moment in time
right there:
where doubletake
and a single exposure
collide.

Safe Passage

Like the aftershocks
of an earthquake in the womb
she feels those moments
of treachery:
men grabbing her father,
her mother's silent screams.

Waves like towers of memory,
push her toward a world
where she will have to respond
or find herself alone.

A blanket tried to replace
that perfect warmth
where she floated weightless
in a sea without time.

Gasping for air
was challenge and promise,
her lips parted
and she heard the word *stand*
sounding a pulsing pride.

Soon she will face *keeping up*
and other expectations
measured by the first of many rules,
and learn that only resistance
will bring her back to herself:
cold breath and fierce identity.

The lingering question is
the choice she didn't know she had:
submit or assume the fight.

It took her years to learn
this language:
words and how she moves her body
will be her safe passage now.

Matching Temperatures

(Mother and Daughter)

Her eyes are two pools
of dark water
reflecting the longing in lives
of matching temperature.

I reach down, she up,
her small hand enclosed
in the pain of one
roughened by work
and arthritic memory.

A child once more,
her sixty years and my ninety
collapse beneath the weight
of these dual yearnings

and every hungry place
where she looked for me
or I for her
trips on our story:
opens wounds no breath can heal.

We keep walking,
hand in hand,
becoming smaller and smaller
until we lose sight of ourselves
in this shudder of dream
that forgets where we meet
and robs one of the sleep
she can no longer give the other.

One of the Lucky Ones

In her city's Central Park *solidarity*
wasn't a word but a warm feeling
soaking her skin with a temperature
she learned in a classroom
of thousands.

Her first child was born at
All Saints Medical Center,
its hidden garden their secret place
when he was four
and the colors of butterflies
were painted by a hand
they imagined together.

Unable to write the unforeseeable
on her daily calendar,
she dressed in familiar clothing,
sure nothing could disrupt
days that became weeks
and weeks years.

But that life diminished
one day to the next,
receded until it disappeared
through the back window of a car
that took her from all she knew.
Exile is now a word
in an unknown language
begging for silence.

She always said she would return
one day when danger
stopped taunting her
from the edges of memory.

Someday, when things were better
and brutal hands no longer
threatened to grab her,
pin her to a time already dead.

Many years passed and she did return,
only to find once familiar streets
leading nowhere
and the houses where she'd lived
changed places with one another.

That's when she understood
escape hadn't made her
one of the lucky ones,
only a woman with pages missing
from her book of life,
a taste forever foreign
in her mouth,
faded images fleeing her eyes.

Refugee

At the close of the journey
there is no finish line,
only a feedback loop.

Days, months,
from one place to the next,
learning new words
to be able to ask and answer,
then forward again,
reaching for refuge,
dragging what matters
and what sticks to the soles
of his feet like a message
from another planet.

Familiar scent of the name
he said he'd never forget
but can no longer remember.

Even black beans simmering
with a choice ham hock
shed bitter tears.

Eternal wanderer
until the last door closes
on daylight and,
shackled,
he stares from the window
of the plane that carries him
past landmarks
that loomed as walls
when he approached them on foot.

Back to where it all began:
to a home
now welcoming as death.

Keep Out

That bully sign proclaiming
this home or land is private,
Keep Out,
powers shaky egos
as it writes each new chapter
in this long story
of us and them.

I remember
when drinking fountains
and lunch counters
screamed *Whites Only*
to our shame
and *Men Only* kept us out
of their private clubs.

Always a target:
Women or those
who refuse our labels,
the dark-skinned
speaking languages
we cannot bother to learn,
or coming from places
we disparage but claim to own.

This line like a bleeding wound
needs more than a sign
and we build an insurmountable wall,
guard it with guns
and innocent dogs
to keep the undesirables
from setting foot
on land we took from their parents.

And when that border is a beach
we call our policy *Dry Foot Wet Foot*,
sending a mixed message
to those seeking only refuge:
welcoming some
while letting others drown.

Sure, we'll make exceptions
for laborers willing to do the jobs
too hard for hands
we only stain with the blood
of the other,
then throw out
when the harvest ends.

You can stay a while
if you work our fields,
care for our children,
clean our shit,
feed our gluttony
or come up with
five million dollars
to buy a bogus belonging.

But wait, maybe
we'll let your children stay
and send you back.
We, who pretend
to honor the family,
rip families apart
as we skewer them in fear.

I want to know when and where
Keep Out first appeared
on our human journey,
who was the first to insult humanity
with those words that lift the few
by banishing the many?

Apartheid lines
drawn by racist gods,
illicit money, and nation states:
all bloating the conceit of those
who cannot imagine themselves
without *Keep Out* as their shield.

National Pastime

Slam dunk, down for the count,
or Hail Mary pass,
the legend sports its superstar logo.

He grew up with that language:
comfortable as scripture
for every day of the week.

A boy, he watched and learned
the best players never attack the face
or any uncovered body part.

Practice meant grooming: rehearsing
sorry and *it won't happen again*
as if he meant it.

If needed, a few locker-room tears,
in private of course
and no one the wiser.

Choosing well was also important
if he aimed to avoid
taking one for the team.

If her father is a member of the club
he knew he would have
an easier time,

a mask for full protections
and his fast ball
would score every time.

With Flowers and Sympathy

He expected a litany
of *yeses* but
she only answered *why*
A rare *no*
might escape her lips
in a whisper
only she could hear.

The words he forced her
to memorize
before bedtime
came back at him
in a volley that had him
setting better traps.

He demanded a vocabulary
for everyday
and another for holidays.

She fought back by
practicing a language
he didn't understand
until one day
she flicked a switch
and spewed a stream
of meaningless gibberish.

They called it a major stroke,
something about
that part of the brain
where speech lives.

His home court advantage
threatened her voice
with every serve
leading her to resort to a win
that took even her
by surprise.

Family and friends
visit her hospital bed
with flowers and sympathy.

They insist they've heard
about cases where the brain
retrains itself
while she pretends oblivion,
enjoying a peace
she never knew before.

Querencia

For Levi Romero

I grew up on this land
stolen once and again
before landing
on conquest's side
of that quivering line.

I heard the word uttered softly,
ancestral and virgin,
by people strong in spirit
who love where they live
whoever claims possession.

Yet it took me a lifetime
of listening
to understand all it means:
attachment to land and people,
or, more simply, love.

In the language
of northern New Mexico
querencia says it all.

1984

After years testing my wings,
exploring the world,
inhabiting other cultures
and giving birth to children
who grew up in places
where I'm from somewhere else,
I came home in 1984.

I never thought about Orwell's book
as prophecy,
a message I didn't understand
with its ominous warning,
digits flashing like a cop car,
sirens blaring,
coming for our future.
settling for our now.

Today we struggle to inhabit
the deliberate chaos
employing brutality to threaten life
and we search for resistance
in the public common,
inside every private prayer
and all those hidden places
no one wants to name.

A prophecy that disrupts
the balance I've nurtured
with my life.
1984 remains a neon glare
at winter's quiet dawn,
a place to honor the writer
and his warning flare.

If I Told You

If I told you
I fell in love with a painting
and lusted after another
would you smile weakly
or invite me to every museum
within my radius of desire?

Loving our children
more than ourselves
is nature's gift to those
healthy enough to live
in a world where sun and moon
dance life's convoluted cycles.

When old people—and I mean
really old,
shuffling through their eighties
or nineties—
speak of physical loving
beyond slivers of soft memory,
the young often shudder
and turn away.

They may be embarrassed,
can't imagine
sensual touch on skin
blotched with liver spots
or caressing see-through hair
baring a scalp of tender pink.

If I tell you I love my person
more than I did when we met
and we were middle-aged then,
taste her changing beauty
as when we hiked together,
our strong legs matched,

that our friendly temperatures
rise and fall together
in a passion of our own invention,
and the courage to create
a scenario that works
is an exciting addition
to the table of periodic elements,

if I told you all that,
would you laugh
and speak of metaphor,
assume, assume,
with nothing to back you up
but paradigms of empty cliché
strangled by fawning glut?

I pity those who trust
convention's lazy eye
over what they feel and know,
content to color within the lines
when the fields beyond
are bright with fireflies
lighting the darkest sky.

Out of an Ochre Haze

For Greg and Rich

Out of an ochre haze
the sun clings to the horizon,
struggles to show us her face,
reassure us clear skies will return.

As so often happens,
dirt reveals truth,
allows us to look directly
at what danger tries
to hide from sight.

Out of a haze that strangles words
and stops feet in their tracks,
this blanket of sand and dust
tells us we must wait.

Weather is always a warning
to our better selves,
a message we receive
or ignore by closing eyes and hearts.

Now the sky disappears
with every other signpost
memory uses
to point us toward home.

She is telling us
This time it's different
but her warning,
offered as grace,
falls on indifferent ears.

Through this ochre haze
some will recognize themselves
walking backward through history
while others hurry to catch up.

Right Where You Hid It to Keep It Safe

Grab your coat, said the phantom in your dream,
it's cold where we're going.
The words rattle the inner walls of your skull
long after waking.

Other lessons and warnings
contradict that crack shot
piercing the border between sleep
and the busyness of day.

You know it is getting warmer fast
in all the most dangerous places
when Greenlanders speak of young ice
too late in the season.

Unlike the dictators of these times,
nature obeys not only money
but loss of memory
and all the magicians have lost their jobs.

Direction no longer holds meaning.
The words *next year*
or *before your grandchild reaches her first birthday*
have succumbed to our sad indifference.

The voice in your dream
doesn't belong to a ghost
but to your conscience,
temporarily lost,
then rediscovering itself
marking time
right where you tried to keep it safe.

Patience in the Eye of the Storm

Tomorrow comes tiptoeing
in trepidation,
fearing two-hundred-mile-an-hour winds
and freezing temperatures.

No calendar promised us
time would be easy,
no guarantee of a safe pass
or danceable music.

We ask the impossible of years
when all our ancestors
taught patience
in the eye of the storm.

A lifetime may unwind
in the length of time it takes
for a tear to run down the cheek
of a condemned man

while breath holds uselessly
as poison hisses through
the pipes in an execution chamber
made to reward vindictive hearts.

Like tailings from a mine,
it's the end of a sentence
tired of its weight in the world,
its unfinished task.

Heirloom Seeds

I planted the heirloom seeds
loving hands stored
from generation to generation,
expected fruit more succulent and sweeter
than those strawberries
from the fields of Irapuato
appearing on my computer screen
the moment my credit card
registers a purchase of anything red.

After buying a pair of Levis online
for weeks I get alluring offers
of every brand:
stretch, new, distressed,
pre-faded or ripped at the knee,
produced in sweatshops
from Taiwan to Oshkosh.

A simple perusal of kitchen knives
floods my inbox with steel
of every cutting edge and strength.

The heirloom seeds refuse to sprout
in a world where water
has lost its fight for survival
and the calendar promises hate
instead of spring.

They prefer to wait underground
until those who plant
and hope to reap
change the direction of prevailing winds
by refusing to dig such early graves.

Best Friend and Alter Ego

I never wanted Raggedy Ann and Andy,
was too young for Barbie and Ken
whose anorexic profiles
would have been out of place
in a home trying not to be Jewish
while stumbling over its name.

Boy dolls seemed beside the point
in any case.
A girl doll was the mirror
where I could change my look
at whim,
repurposing features
as they went in and out of style.

My only doll was Heather
and she gave me all she had,
was best friend and alter ego,
her humble presence
soothing every trick played
on my young life.

Small, rag-stuffed
and of indeterminate age,
she didn't protest
when I gave her the name
I wanted for myself:
its syllables speaking winner
in every popularity fest.

One day, in a fashion tantrum
I cut her brown wool locks
then gave her redemption
with yellow hair
to match the fifties mood
that always felt like the party
I wasn't invited to.

Heather accompanied me
to the hospital
when doctors laid me open
and probed my child's body.
She slept with me
at home or on the road,
calming my darkest fears.

No nose job possible
on a one-dimensional face,
and she imbued me
with the courage to laugh off
the one my mother prescribed
when I was old enough.

That *old enough* never arrived
like the other dreams
my mother longed to live
through me,
and Heather disappeared
along with other childhood props
when she'd outlived the pitfalls
of our one-sided friendship.

By then I'd given her freckles,
covered them with rosy cheeks,
repainted her face
so often it lost all symmetry.
I sometimes think of her
wherever dolls go to die
and the beautiful friendship we had.

Witness

*Written on the 80th anniversary of the
liberation of Auschwitz-Birkenau,
January 27, 2025*

Witness from this distant place
explodes at a different temperature
of pain
when the figure of a loved one
appears on its horizon.

Evil as indelible lesson
fades on a landscape
sewn with seeds
of newly minted hate.

We may tell the story,
preserve it for those
whose memory is woven
from our words.

But when victim becomes victimizer
and mother, lover, child
are the protagonists,
what was never supposed
to happen again
breaks down the door
and witness becomes
a different exercise:

this cracked dish that once held
the kugel he loved,
the threadbare shawl
that covered her shoulders,
a single glove looking for its mate
or a doll with one eye
descending its cheek like a tear.

When what we see is ours
it's no longer only witness
but a flame devouring that page
of the family Bible
inscribed with precise names,
specific dates.

Roberta Flack (1937-2025)

When we sort all those trains
careening along the narrow-gauge tracks
that crisscross the rocky playing fields
of our minds,
horizons will open on every side,
trees grow
and language reach the end of the line
where everyone must get off.

Will we hurry on home,
each carrying our sorrows
to the single-family dwelling
where every task starts at zero,
every footprint disappears in sand
and every kiss feels like the last?

Or will we gather on that platform,
glad for one more chance
to raise our voices in the final chorus
of *The First Time Ever I Saw Your Face*
accompanied by the full-throated voice
of one who walked softly
and bequeathed us the gift of music
in the bag she left beneath her seat?

There Will Be Room for Breath

It may require persuasion
but if you can convince the gag reflex
to abandon center stage,
there will be room for breath
to take its place.

Seasons of sun will rise then,
confident in the sky,
flooding you and those you love
with the warmth of their embrace.

Keeping hurt from installing
itself in your gut
is a task young girls confront
before they can speak their names.

Chasing submission
from ground zero
at the base of your spine
takes a community
cheering you on.

The hollow of your throat
is no place to harbor indecision
or the debris we collect along the way.

Shame is the devil's advocate
always ready to crowd you out,
a shapeshifter reinventing itself
at every turn.

The only way to guard against
this cast of bully imposters
is to call on memory
and start fighting back
before they track you down.

We Hold Hands

For Emma Nahuí Álvarez Randall

We hold hands across three generations,
this great granddaughter and me.

A neon connection travels my aging body
to her elastic one,
what once was me
races to catch up
with the woman she will be.

A Lego tower reaches beyond the ceiling
in this room where she plays.

Perfect words in her deliberate hand
fill the page of her second-grade workbook.
Her strong body pumps the park swing
to a horizon of clouds.

Pink, pink, pink,
is there anywhere in the world
where little girls don't love pink,
dress pink, want everything pink?

Yet she stands tall to peer through
a telescope at Saturn's rings,
closes one eye
as she presses the other
to the microscope
in search of the crease
in a beetle's knee.

She dreams of becoming a doctor
like her mother,
never imagines herself a nurse.

At this family gathering
she makes the rounds
with a serving platter,
offers small slices of blood sausage
and French bread,
repeats the name of the delicacy
as she moves from guest to guest.

I take two,
letting my swollen fingers
graze the sweet warmth
of her limber ones.

When she rushes to take my arm
to guide me up the stairs
it is more than physical help
and I long to know the math she juggles
as she deposits me at the top.

Too soon,
I will no longer be here
and she will continue to grow
into the woman who may one day
become a great grandmother
who thinks her own great grandchildren
the most amazing, brilliant
and generous of them all.

For now, I strain to hear the story
she is telling her brother,
making it up as she goes along.
The one that ends:
And they died happily ever after!

What Is Life

For Julia

What is life, she asks
her older cousin
and he answers in a language
only they understand.

As she learns more
she will forget what she brought
with her into a world
that kills its own.

I wish her words
that play well
with memory.

A Periodic Table of Personal Elements

Early, they stole trust from you,
so early it never had a chance
to bloom in that place
where a periodic table
of personal elements
waits to be consulted.

Through all our years,
you asked it to come to your aid,
show us it lives
in the words you whisper in my ear.

Loving me as you do,
you wanted to trust,
peel terror back
like the layers of an onion,
leaving nothing behind.

Loving you as I do,
I thought if I removed my mask
you might meet me at that place
where sandstone spires
reach for sky.

But the suffocating wall
they built to keep you fearful, apart,
believing if you let down your guard
betrayal was ready to pounce,
kept screeching *Don't... don't...*

That dissonant message assaulted you
by force at night
and by day stood ever ready
to pick you up and run.

You are tired now, so tired.
The sickness has done its work
and ability flees
leaving you with a muddy road ahead.

There is nothing to do but peel
the onion's layers
until all that remains is feeling,
raw and honest
in a you that belongs to you.

Understanding I Don't Understand

The dark shadow approaches
on menacing feet,
familiar trick.

You feel it coming
but never know where or when.
And like all shadows,
its heart follows its own beat.

No words can define it,
none that are known
to those who have never felt its chill.
No telltale sound or scent
remains as evidence.

I say I understand and know I don't.
I say I understand I don't understand
and my words dissolve in brittle air.

Fiction can't spell its name
or hold its memory
where we see it
in the transparency of a clear fall day,
or reflected on motionless water.

To block out the sun,
we can turn away or cover our eyes
with two fingers' worth of fear.
Breath dares not argue with wind
where legacy lives.

This distance turns on me
and multiplies.
Its temperature freezes me out,
then brings me face to face
with that answerless question.

You stand in your pain, unable to speak
or feel my touch,
this crescendo of promise
made from the distant shore
of a vast sea.

I am here but invisible to your history
of choosing life
despite all the signposts
meant to undermine your genes,
leading you away from yourself.

Perhaps one day
you will leave the pain behind,
move into a place
where you believe you are safe.

But then again,
perhaps you won't.

Facts

*Come one, come all
to the circus
of doom,
all three rings offering
a star-spangled gala
for those of every age!*

The ringmaster changes maps,
boasts he can kill
and get away with it.
The audience is in awe.

Clowns punctuate his repertoire,
fawning about him,
their sad grins
painted red, white, and blue.

The audience laughs.
Sitting so close
and it's the greatest show
on earth.

*Come one, come all
to the circus
of doom,
all three rings offering
a star-spangled gala
for those of every age!*

Now the ringmaster
cracks his whip,
taunts the women in the stands,
promises to deport all immigrants,
expel the gender-different
from their lives,
ridicules those with disabilities
as he shouts:
I will make America great again!

Gross advertisement
for hatred and revenge,
he erases a good neighbor legacy
and promotes a culture
born in our ability
to make ourselves big
by making others small.

He favors walls over bridges,
doesn't believe
climate change is real,
has no thought for tomorrow.

You too can join this circus.
The first in line
will get to choose
between their very own cage
and a spot between the bearded lady
and Siamese twins
joined at the hip
in the sideshow of freaks.

Just leave your integrity
on that pile of shorn hair
and gold teeth,
sign here and hurry along.

*Come one, come all
to the circus
of doom,
all three rings offering
a star-spangled gala
for those of every age!*

The ringmaster's lies
are transparent
yet the facts exist
for everyone to see.
But facts, once honored,
have lost their battle with trickery.

In an age when the patriarch's boot
shatters reason
and feeds its excess food
to those who are starved for truth,
what isn't is,
and what is
will destroy us all.

*Come one, come all
to the circus
of doom,
all three rings offering
a star-spangled gala
for those of every age!*

A Know-It-All Conceit

My computer wants to introduce me
to Copilot,
an entity it insists knows more
about writing than me.

I've tried asking several versions
of AI
a question or two
and found their answers
embarrassing.

Like Siri and Alexis before them,
know-it-all conceit
stands in for knowledge
and imagination.

I don't want their help,
prefer this voice I've grown
through every season,
this style that expresses the me of me.

No Luddite, I welcomed spellcheck
to my repertoire.
Cut and paste has earned my gratitude.
But enough is enough.

My cellphone suffers from ADHD,
no longer waits for my commands
but races ahead,
anticipating nonexistent need.

The saccharine voice that tells me
press one if you're a patient,
two if a doctor or three a pharmacy
can't count high enough
to satisfy my simple longing
for a human
at the other end of the line.

I go to sleep each night
fearing another loss of autonomy,
wake each morning
wary of the genie that wants
to insinuate itself
between my creativity and me.

Nostalgia for the fountain pen
and rotary phone
tickle my memory.

This thing called progress
is like an entitled male
who believes whiter,
richer and stronger
is sure to win every race.

They Think They Know

They think they know
what we're up to
and we don't tell them
think again,
the pathways of their minds
twisted as they are.

Or they couldn't care less
what we do and say,
as sideshow mirrors
project their reflections
onto a sea of compliant lips
spewing *pretty little woman*
in hopeful tone.

Some of my best friends are...,
I understand,
and other such clichés
may seem benign
to the youthful ear,
but we have memory
on our side.

We were born beyond their reach
and grew feral in the recesses
of their formal gardens.
Our seed is resistant to promises
crafted of intimidation,
coercion and lies.

They came bearing gifts
enticingly wrapped
in paper embossed with glitter
and cheerful holiday scenes,
tied with ribbons
that sparkle and seduce.

But we have plenty of gifts
of our own creation
made by the tools of our trade,
a taste for food
that nourishes and heals.

And our gifts multiply
on nights when they've fallen
into a stupefied sleep
contagious as the plague
before we dared imagine hope.

Let them think
what keeps them feeling big,
allows them to redraw borders
through power and fear
and believe they are safe
in their forever greed.

When they feel most secure
we will appear
in some ordinary season:
legions ready to imprison them
in a cage of their own design
and throw away the key.

Every Step Forward Brings Ghostly Images

I rail against easy-speak and fake-speak,
turn my back on autofill,
readymade messages,
emoticons that erase the texture of voice
and dismantle imagination.

And I think of Socrates
five hundred years before our era,
scoffing at the written word
because he believed it killed dexterity,
replaced the mind's muscle
with texts that live
where memory belongs.

From oral to written,
books in an edition of one
to reproduction that multiplied
recipients of the story,
from the slow impression
of a flatbed press
to digital repetition
and the infinite knowledge
of cyberspace,
we move at the speed of light.

But what do we lose on this journey
to progress,
what do we cast aside
when we leap ahead,
not stopping to savor the old
while celebrating the new?

Every step forward
brings ghostly images
of who and where we were
while each memory
holds all seasons
in its generous hands.

Own the Trouble

When horror overwhelms,
pressing in on all sides,
grabbing and choking
as it tries to reduce us
to trembling pawns in its game,
you must call on memory
to remind you who you are.

This is no time to obey
in advance,
imagine acquiescence will save us
or going along
keep us from trouble.

Own the trouble,
subvert and defeat it
to save yourself
and memory.

This is not the first time a psychopath
feeds evil to those he believes
he controls,
would have us chew,
digest and feed it to our young.

Not the first. Not the last.
And we are still here,
resisting,
the only currency
that insures a future
where love may spar with hate
and win.

The Day Before

The day before is unseasonably ripe,
rough edges pitted
by worry and shaky breath.

We live in a conclave of Coriolis force,
spilling into the other hemisphere
when asked too much of it.

I live north of the equator
but my heart is divided
between identical twins.

One listens for the other's steady pulse
in her sleep,
murmurs words of comfort
in her ear.

The other, more adventurous,
may pretend oblivion,
a transparent plea for attention.

Nothing to do but let go,
close my eyes
and dream of the world we deserve.

My Voice

My voice cracks
from the weight of years,
sometimes needs a few seconds
to get from thought to word
or follow the music's beat.

It has left the eager decibels
of adolescent angst behind,
doesn't aspire to glory
or a unique place
in its lifetime of robust speech.

It may careen against these walls
erected to keep it in its place,
stumble over the barricades
of earlier wars,
let others fill the void.

But do not be fooled.
My voice still knows
where it's going,
journeys on roads discernible
on ancient maps.

It has learned to join every voice
in all the languages
born from our insatiable need
to tell it like it is.

It doesn't seek the spotlight
but takes its place
in this rhythmic chant
that will deafen all attempts
to silence or kill it off.

Lies

We tell them
because we are afraid,
to get ahead
or not be left behind—
which may seem like the same
but isn't.

We tell them to feel powerful,
then repeat them
to strangle doubt.

We are told it is wrong
by those who don't want us
to notice them practicing
their own smooth coverups
or exaggerated tales.

Lies of commission
and omission,
lies that only want
to make you feel good
and those some call white,
implying no harm done:
racialized words
on negligent lips.

A lifetime of small lies
prepares you
to ignore the one
that is killing you
as you sleep,
hidden like the forest
we cannot see
when only looking
at the tree.

And that is the lie you
bequeath your children
who will bequeath it
to theirs
until truth doesn't
makes us proud
and words no longer
mean what they say.

The Genius of Lime

In Asia, rice anchors meals
for thousands of years,
gathered by bent backs
and blind hands
in the depths of watery fields.

Corn plays the same role
on tables throughout the Americas
from cobs chewed dry in antiquity
to tortillas:
rounds of nixtamal formed
by millennia of women's hands
and baked on clay
with the genius of lime
fashioning a staple
that keeps pellagra at bay
nurturing health
one generation to the next.

Beans, too, are ancient foods:
their rainbow varieties
simmering in pots over embers,
wood, electricity or gas:
a fuel for every age.

These foods tell origin stories
repeated around tables
to ears as willing as mouths:
food as sustenance
against our infestation of loss.

The Integrity of Fire

In the year 213 before our era,
Alexander sought every book
for the library that bore his name.
In that same year
the Chinese Emperor Shihungdi
burned those his thought police
found among the subjects
of his realm.

His rampage raged from door to door,
village to village,
erasing all history before himself.

Fire embraces cones
with their scent of pine,
revels in cedar breath
as the seasons turn,
willingly metamorphizes to coal
spread beneath ritual cuts of meat
sizzling on communal grills
but refuses to devour the pages
of a book
if it has the choice.

Burning books
insults the integrity of fire
as it fights our hunger for ideas
and magical travels through lands
born in the imaginations of others
to be nurtured by our own
and passed from writer to reader:
gifts of every age.

Pyres of books
are always a prelude to danger,
sad forerunner to larger ovens,
fascist onslaught
repeating itself on any stage
in every century,
fear and confidence
reenacting the struggle
that would chain our minds
or set them free.

Shihuangdi wanted history
to begin with him.
His decree was implacable
and those who resisted
were buried alive
along with their families.
No one was spared.

Today the courageous stories
that tell us who we are
go up in flame again,
their pages reduced
to ashes of shame.

Every era has its murderers
of words,
those frightened of dreams,
intimidated by future.
Fire itself can only cry out
with the pain of the innocent.

Adding a Piece to the Puzzle

A word is spoken,
an event takes place
and the clock
begins its countdown.

Each year that passes
takes you farther
from its taste, smell,
the truth it told.

We remember at our peril
but forgetting is worse
because it lets the enemy
in the door.

Close your eyes
and wait for recognition
to build a ladder of trust.

If nothing else,
you will add a piece
to that puzzle
waiting to be whole.

An Arrow Hit Its Mark

Fly beneath the radar,
they told us,
don't make waves,
and *men don't marry
smart women.*

I listened with
all the fervor
of teenage trust,
did my best
to do my worst.

Then an arrow
hit its mark
right in the center
of my yearning
breast.

Its point,
dipped in threat,
dragged my dreams
through this course
of obstacles.

That's when I soared
just above
the horizon,
shouting *here I am*
to the four directions.

My daughters know
they are smart
and my son honors
the hidden brilliance
of women.

My legacy's lesson is:
never listen
to that bully chorus
meant to erase us
from our lives.

Transitions

I stop, immobile,
wait until where I was is gone
and where I'm going
is more than a spot
on the far horizon.
Transitions are juggling acts
for me now.

No, I'm not talking about
that kind of transition,
mine's not about identity.
I'm still who I've always been,
she and *her* are my pronouns
and I decline to use
the honorific *Doctor*
before my name.

I've never been tempted
to get a tattoo
or dye my hair green.
A skullcap of thinning white
has long since replaced
my chestnut mane.
I live in reliable jeans
and a simple black shirt
but my every transition
is deliberate now.

Moving from sleep to wakefulness
I take my time,
reluctant to leave that warm cocoon
and face head-on
the rising hunger of each day.

Even that most mundane of transitions
from cold to heat,
greeting a friend from years ago
whose name I've forgotten,
or considering whether
to challenge a rude remark
not aimed at me.

Where I once leapt
with youth's abandon
I now slow way down,
savor the moment,
take its measure,
contemplate choice
and consequence.

Today's bridges are more tenuous,
broken in places,
smelling of danger
as often as they point the way
to the next discovery
on this exuberant journey.

The bundle of memories
on my back is still tied
with brightly colored ribbons
but rests on sagging flesh
and tired bone.

Dreams that once seduced,
cajoled or tickled,
stare back
from this desert landscape
that is my map.
Some wink
while others laugh out loud.

Lifeboat, ladder:
one more gift of age
I was too busy to inhabit
when young:
a liminal space I now explore
with grateful curiosity.

Christmas 2024

A day believed holy by some,
profitable to others
or a moment for privileged families
to unite around tables
weighted with surplus.

Some will try to avoid conversation
that may disrupt the fictitious joy
so prized this time of year.

Other neighborhoods burst out
in a seasonal carol
as those without homes
seek the manger in the myth.

In Ukraine, hope freezes
like blood on heavy snow.
No celebration for Gaza
in its silence of death.

Nicaragua, once a nation
devoted to the Virgin,
searches for her image
in exiled churches now.

This year,
the first day of Chanukah
falls on Christmas day
or Christmas falls
on the first day of Chanukah:
similar prayers
speak words of praise
and deception.

Muslims, Buddhists
and those of every faith
insist their sacred stories
unite and heal,
not dominate or destroy.

Like every year in every place,
a parenthesis of ritual
stands in for what might be
instead of this halo of lies.

A Garden of Possibility

The newborn with air to breathe
cradles expectation
that sprouts: tiny shoots at first,
then becomes a garden
of possibility.

Where possibility cannot exist
because hunger and pain
have taken their toll,
there is no anticipation,
no new bloom
exciting the seasons.

Regret only lives
where imagination fails
to prepare the soil
and there is no place for hope.

Years may change direction
in any life
but some will be silenced
by a destiny they cannot predict
and no one deserves.

False promises,
fairytales and political lies
collude on maps
not drawn from contours of culture
but by hands
that would only save themselves.

A willingness to risk
and the courage of escape
bring sprouting seeds to the surface,
anticipation on land made barren
by any war
that claims it will end in peace.

Regret becomes a tiny animal then
burrowing deep in the flesh
of those who ask the questions
whose impotent answers
battle our dreams.

Their Up, My Down

> *"El mundo está patas arriba."*
> *(The world is upside down.)*
> —Eduardo Galeano

Blessed art the meek, Jesus said,
for they shall inherit the earth.
And his followers
launched an Inquisition,
waged holy wars and wrote a story
that punishes the meek.

Every religion promises glory
now or in a world to come
as long as we take its Scripture
to be The Word
of a one and only God.

Too many revolutions,
fought in the name of the poor,
pretended justice here on earth
as they drown in a swamp
of corruption.
And here we go again.

Politicians of every stripe
claim they are working for us
as they climb that ladder of power.
No lie too big,
no deceit oblivious to their greed.

I am writing this south of the equator
where their up is my down
and if you dig a hole in your dream
you will land right side up
on the other side of the world.

The answer is always just beyond
the horizon.
All you need are strong legs,
a willing spirit
and truth to break your fall
on the way down.

The Lake

For J

Looking from her window
she can see the lake,
its horizon
separating waves from blue sky.

Every conversation begins
with that lake,
how it draws her eyes
that once caught a gesture
and sketched it in minutes.

As she loses art and word,
the lake takes their place,
fills her empty spaces,
limits this sharp pain of loss.

She is there and the lake
is there,
faithful companion
as she unravels in real time.

Maren

She whose mother once sat
on this very floor
playing with my grandkids,
now parents themselves,
she whose aunt gave me her recipe
for coq au vin
written in her elegant hand.

She who sailed the Galápagos,
hiked each tiny island with us
in search of Darwin's yellow finch
among blue-footed boobies
and marine iguanas sunning themselves
like miniature dinosaurs on volcanic rock,
she is another now.

She who discussed the recent changes
in psychoanalysis
and global political patterns
as only a woman can,
lies motionless in a bed
beside a window with a splendid view
of a garden she may still love.

I take her hand, frail as cosmic dust
inert upon the sheet.
I search her eyes,
the tiny muscles around her mouth
worried by sudden attempts to speak,
trying to find a scrap of shared ground,
some key that might unlock
the world we shared,
some idea or image she still holds.

The man who wooed and won her
seven decades ago
sits beside her now,
his long loss a monument of pain
between them,
his voice resigned yet hopeful
as he ventures *hola*:
brief prayer
failing to spark recognition.

We do not know
he will leave before
she does,
nor whether she will
wave him goodbye.

She is here and not here,
conscious and unconscious
in a space I cannot enter.

Now her lips move and there is sound
but the words lose themselves
on this curious land
that separates where she has gone
from where I struggle to connect.

I reach for any fleeting sense
of where she travels now.

When I stroke her head of gray curls
and tell her I must go,
tears well in her lost eyes
and her mouth forms the word *lindo*,
uttered so softly
I can barely hear its shape.

I want to believe she means our visit,
turn quickly so she won't see
my own eyes
dimmed by rage and sorrow,
and take my leave of this woman
who has moved beyond our common time.

"What I Have Done No One Has Done Before"

With thanks to Irene Vallejo

It's true, the first poem
was written by a woman.
Fifteen hundred years
before the *Iliad* and the *Odyssey*
Enheduanna wrote verses
unknown until now.

Poet and priestess of antiquity,
they call her the Shakespeare
of Sumerian literature:
inevitable comparison
and forerunner
to such gratuitous compliments
as *You write like a man.*

Poems, songs, and the earliest
astronomical notations
are attributed to her.
Her voice echoes in the psalms
of Biblical fame,
refuses to remain hidden,
sounds now
in its recovered power.

Before Homer, before Plato,
long before all those men
we were schooled
to commit to memory,
Enheduanna raised her voice
and sang in my dreams:
her sweet and bitter legacy.

Exiled from a culture that believed
women had no right to speak,
she was cast from her home
and forced to wander,
her journey a map of wounds.

And she continued to write,
proudly claiming:
What I have done no one has done before.

We Whisper Before We Speak

English lived in my mouth
since before I was born
but shifted its powerful body
to welcome Spanish
to the neighborhood.

I've made brief visits
to other tongues
but never long enough
to explore their depths
or discover their secret places.

Still, certain exotic words
find their way to my lips:
some lost direction,
others were curious
or came in celebration.

There are those that project
region or culture
through accent and inflection,
insist they have the same right
as anyone to stay.

Meanwhile,
new generations arrive
bearing sounds
that define new ways of being,
enrich the stew
or probe connection.

We whisper before we speak,
speak before we shout,
shout before we fill the air
with a truth that can topple
any tower of Babel.

The poems I bequeath the world
have room for them all.
They demand the privilege
of singing their truth
to all who stop to listen.

What We Already Know

One of these days a storyteller
sitting astride all those turtles
will plant her magic
in every dream.

When the dreamers wake,
they'll know how to renew
their contracts with life,
practice kindness
and mend the nearest broken heart.

Imagine that morning:
from one day to the next
entitlement will disappear,
nations begin caring for their own
and the rich stop wanting more.

Gradually, toxic waste
and other insults to the earth
will fade,
leaving fields fertile,
mountains whole,
seasons gentle
and air we can inhale.

Stunned, we'll learn
there's enough for everyone
and we can divide it
among everyone
according to need.

Virgin forests will rise proudly
once more,
storms will settle their grievances
and whales will hear
one another's song.

The word *war* won't exist
in any language
and every weapon will become
a musical instrument,
paintbrush, pen, or spoon.

Every skin color,
every gender,
gay and straight,
young and old,
those of every culture
and ability
will feel at home
in a world of reason
and sustenance,
imagination and genius,
passed with pride
through the maternal line.

One day that dream
will penetrate
the porous borders of our fear
and demolish greed
like the rush
of a mighty waterfall.

We can get there
by looking and listening,
standing very still,
opening our eyes
and inhaling the pulsing rhythm
of what we already know.

The Porter

For Enrique Esperón

It's been fifteen years.
I remember my first sight
of the lean man
with muscled arms and quick smile,
his body straining
beneath a box of vegetables,
fruit, meat and cheese
he carried to my son's apartment
two blocks away.

Enrique wasn't the one
who grew the produce,
raised the beef or made the cheese.
He was the porter, heavy lifter,
strong shoulders
at Sunday's street market,
bearer of weight.

If he didn't have to get back
right away,
my son would invite him
to sit a while,
pass the *mate* gourd
and they'd talk about climate:
hot, cold, or political.

When I visited that tiny country
far to the south
I sometimes tagged along
to Sunday market,
met Enrique and wondered
about the man who worked
such a simple job.

One trip I gave a public reading
from my book of poems
for the disappeared,
those men and women
terror plucked from street or home,
never to be seen again.

That country's cold burden
leaving families incomplete
like a warm fabric
eaten away by moths,
pock-marked by grief.

Old memories, forever present
in those left behind,
wounds time won't heal
in the history of a land
that's suffered the cruelty
of dictatorship.

I read that day at the city's
Museum of Memory
to people seated in rows of chairs
holding loss in their laps:
broken families,
empty places at the dinner table,
cheeks still waiting
for their nighttime kiss
or morning smile.

Enrique asked for the day off,
took three buses
from his rural home
to get to my reading on time.
I never asked if he misses someone,
likes poetry, or was simply curious
about what his friend's mother
had to say.

We never spoke of the poems
but ever since
he sends a message to my FB page,
a line or two a couple of times a year
asking how I am.

My son says Enrique
doesn't own a computer,
must go to his daughter's house
to write those lines
as dependable as monsoon rains
in the southern hemisphere.

Enrique, who hoists my son's food
on his shoulder and has become
a face in my wilderness:
one precious voice
in the vast silence of these times.

Your Story

There is a story
woven into the blanket
that cradled your first breath
ready to tell you
where you're from
and where you hope to go.

You are only a minor character,
the protagonist
is a vengeful God
ready to mete out punishment
each time you fail to follow his rules.

As you age,
the story will grow longer,
peopled by those
you are allowed to love and marry,
the number of children
you may have.

The story they say is yours
will name you after its hero,
tell you where you must live
and what to think.

Beware of the stories
told by those who are killing you slowly
while painting you in glowing colors
for their profit or delight.

A story to make you small
or one to keep you afraid,
one that erases your history,
another that changes your name.

Stories that confuse your direction,
leading you to think
you are on a mountain trail
but find yourself
in a crowded city instead.

It may take you a while
but if you keep imagination close
you will discover your own story
when you need it most.

It was written by you
and belongs to you
in the cold of winter
or summer heat.
If you feed it well
it will never let go
of your trusting hand.

Beware those stories meant
to belittle, distract
or lead you away from yourself.
The only story you will ever need
is yours.

Theater of Folly

I am dancing on the head of a pin
remembering a future
where humans obey the wind
and nothing of value is lost.

Curtains are drawn
on this theater of folly,
the hard wooden seats
hurt your bones
and each season promises
more of what we need,
not merely crave.

Their lies will never find
themselves at home
in such a landscape
of pure desire.
No breathable air
can hold them.

I hear the splintering
of glass houses,
fresh grief of breakage
and brittle despair
burning my ears.

There is nothing left
for me to do
but coax memory
to where I have forged a trail
and know there is a place
untouched
by the thunder of boulders
crashing through slot canyons
in the night.

Your Contribution

Once you understand the *why*,
the *how* will appear
clamoring for attention.
You reach for it,
careful to keep your balance.

You must consider what you risk
by doing your work
and what will be lost if you don't.

The *where* is a mirror
you can hold in either hand.
The direction you face
will determine what you remember
a century from now.

That memory, of course,
will no longer belong to you.
It will live in the story
a great granddaughter
tells the child she is teaching
to read in another country,
written in another language.

Your contribution
is suspended equidistant
between history and future,
a pendulum of light
on some dark night
when what we do today
is only a distant memory
yearning to escape its prison
of denial.

We Are We

For Barbara

I peel an orange and cut it
into bite-sized pieces,
add blueberries, strawberries
--hard to find these days
due to climate change
and other human disasters—
add slices of banana
and seasonal fruit.

I boil water in a small pot
and set the timer
for your six-minute egg,
cut a small piece
of the cornbread I make and freeze.
Sometimes you want coffee,
sometimes green tea.

I'll do it again tomorrow.
Preparing your breakfast
is never work, love,
but one small gift
among those I can give.

Yours to me are received in kind:
making sure my glasses
are clean when my poor eyes
fail to see their grime,
running a hot bath on a cold day,
loading my walker into the car.

We never take for granted
these small kindnesses
listed in no division of labor
but nurtured for 39 years
and propelling us into a future
where loving one another
includes anticipating
such needs.

Artistic community,
political agreement,
love of family
and physical attraction
brought us together.

They are the larger contours
of our relationship:
bedrock and continuity.
But it's these small gestures
evoking my daily gratitude
that remind me we are we.

Nothing for Tomorrow

At eighty-nine, I think of readiness
differently,
leave no task unfinished.

I don't want anything undone
in case something happens
and no time remains.

And yes, the something on my mind
is death,
a major stroke or unexpected fall.

After a lifetime of perfect flights,
will this plane be the one
to go down?

Will I see the end before it comes
or will it surprise me
in my sleep?

I have spoken my piece,
have no debts,
and am up to date with my bills.

The final versions of next year's books
are in my publisher's hands,
proofs corrected, covers approved.

I've told my children, grandchildren,
great grandchildren,
a few dear friends
and you
what you mean to me.

Ready as I can be
for that final destination,
I'm leaving nothing
for tomorrow.

Tomorrow

Tomorrow avoids our eyes
and shrugs her shoulders
when we ask too much of her.

She's never really liked her name,
would have preferred
something less pretentious,
better suited to these times.

I admit I enjoy teasing the word
that keeps me
in suspense each night
and surprises me
with every welcome sunrise.

Two can play this game.
I will ignore her threats
and take her irony in stride.

For now, I just say:
Come on, Tomorrow,
at this late date
don't try to fool me
with your silly games.

The Butcher's Dishonest Thumb

Suffering only from those conditions
of age that kill imperceptibly,
when I say *I could go at any time*
it's conjecture, not intention.

It doesn't gnaw at me like a hunger
that must be fed three times a day,
more like a vague itch I scratch
but fail to calm.

A riddle hovering in the wings,
shy and sometimes taunting,
it has yet to discover my secret places
though not for lack of trying.

And it's precisely its shadowy presence
that feels like the butcher's
dishonest thumb on the scale:
a question that may be answered
tomorrow or decades down the road,
floating sharp-edged
but weightless in my hands.

All I can know for sure:
I won't be here for the great reveal,
won't know if it came sooner,
later, or how.

Definition

Ernesto "Che" Guevara, 1928-1967

What should I call him, Fidel asked
as he bid farewell
to his comrade-in-arms.

The plaza was full.
People struggled to breathe
in the heat of that heaving mass.

Artist was the word he chose
for the Argentine doctor
who saw injustice and met it
where it lived.

Not *revolutionary*, never *general*,
he sought a word
that describes the depths
of compassion and commitment
of one who gave his life
for those who know only misery.

Artist,
a word that ignites the tongue
with combustible medicine
to cure what we do not want to see.

Artist, that place where risk
and imagination
meet in this dance called life.

Swimming in Defeat

You are on a crowded street
and suddenly realize
you are naked.
Nowhere to hide.
We've all had that dream.

As I age, I dream awake,
predicaments too close
to reality,
rooted in the dangers
that invade my hope.

In one, a stroke or accident
has robbed me
of my right hand
and I must train the left
to do its job.

Will there be time enough
to cultivate that dexterity
I 've nurtured
through this lifetime
of try and fail?

In another, summer is here
and the words
I've tended with pride
have fled my garden.

Can I finish this poem
and those to come
before the last one leaves me
swimming in defeat?

Smoke Signals

*Written after the conclave of May 7 and 8, 2025,
to choose a new Roman Catholic pope.*

The smoke issuing from that chimney
atop the chapel
where Michelangelo left a sliver of space
between the fingers of God and man
rises black or white
announcing the dramatic wait continues
or a new pope is named.

According to the fable,
he will be the reincarnation
of St. Peter
instructing 1.4 billion Catholics
in punishment and reward,
telling them what to believe,
who they may love and marry
and how many children to have.

Some say that sliver of space
represents free will
but there is no room for freedom
when St. Peter's descendant speaks.

Inside the chapel
133 cadmium-robed men
—always men—
paint politics as faith,
trade favors, count votes,
impose obedience
and claim the decision
is guidance from above.

This is no honest messaging
like the puffs of smoke
created by rhythmic fanning of flame
among North America's first peoples
calling across vast divides.

Nor smoke signals warning of danger
from tower to tower
along the 13-mile meander
of China's Great Wall,
not those the Yámana of Brazil
send up,
inviting people
to share the meat of a whale
that's washed ashore.

These men,
proclaimed holy
by a church that launched
a conquest of death,
carried out the Crusades,
burned courageous women at the stake
and protects the abusers of children,
have turned the teachings
of a humble Jewish sage
into the law of heaven and earth
bedecked in silks and gold.

In today's Rome the faithful pray,
wave flags and cheer
when the smoke from that chimney
turns white.

A new pope has been chosen
and the world's press
writes his story
in line with the interests
that pay their wages of sin.

Let us rouse cleansing winds
to shatter that arrogance
and hurl such edicts
back in the faces of those
who would choke us
with ancient superstition
revived.

When the Countdown Begins

The defiant final season
like any curtain call
may come for us
when we least suspect
its thunder.

We may not even hear that roar
rumbling on a frequency
beyond the desert hum
of audible imagination.

I don one mask after another
stored in airtight vaults
at the department of props.
All are too heavy
or lack holes for eyes.

One mask opens to reveal
another smaller one
within its ancient song.
Will it fit my face,
contorted by trying
to keep the lies at bay?

Until one morning I wake
wearing a mask that fits.
It was specially designed
to register my name
while erasing my identity.

In some distant galaxy a race
of beings we've always pictured
in grotesque error
laugh at our naiveté.

This may be a grandiose dream
crowding gentler ones,
an exercise in endurance
or supporting act
in the circus coming to town.

Buy your tickets now
or risk being left behind.
When the countdown begins
you won't want to stand
on the sidelines of history.

But remember, you can always
use your most powerful voice,
outshout the chorus,
scream until you are heard
by every god invented
to bully your true identity
in the swamp reserved
for those who grovel as they
usher in this hologram of doom.

No Thank You

Deep into my nineth decade,
I've been writing since I learned how.
I was six
and delighted in creating little stories
copied in my child's hand
and distributed in the neighborhood.

Since then, I've honed my craft,
paid attention to those places
where meaning meets form
in this magical symphony
called language.
Reaching for originality,
I ignore those modalities
designed to imprison me.

Just as I disdain Hallmark,
prefer to pen greetings
free of scripted holidays,
reject the suggestions
offered by readymade verse
and emoticons intruding upon my style,
I resent these new phantoms
calling themselves AI, ChatGPT
or Copilot each time
I enter Microsoft Word.

No thank you.
I'd rather fly solo.

Help where no help is needed
is like the husband
who finishes your sentences,
the neighbor who rings your bell
and peers past you
when you open the door,
or any aid that reduces us
to the desperation of cliché.

Invisible wizard of these times:
if you're short on ideas
to make our lives easier,
let me suggest a few:

You could start
by putting an end
to wars and violence.
Devise a way for everyone
to have a place to live
and food to eat.
Bring back critical thinking,
currently disparaged
but necessary for survival.

And if those are beyond you,
simple kindness to those in need
would be a start.

Mother's Day

> *"My veins do not end in me."*
> —Roque Dalton

A special day? Really?
Only one out of 365
when connection
threatens danger?

My blood pulses in the veins
of son and daughters,
a grandchild's eyes
carry my curiosity.

In their children
—my greats—
a gesture may appear in profile
laughing at my sorry demand.

Blood makes itself at home
one generation to the next
but other essences
also vie for the prize.

Not biology
but a radius of desire
and the ability to pronounce
its own name.

The mentor who colors
outside the lines,
the teacher you remember
because she saw you
when others looked away.

The one who creates against
prevailing winds,
uncovers a secret or treads a path
not marked on any map.

Woman, man, or any gender:
all are mothers
in the deepest meaning
of that word.

Listen to the Silence

For Greg and Rich

A poem is crafted of words
this house resists,
its silence tells us
images are the story
when morning travels
its luminous path to knowing.

The white that bathes these walls
isn't paint
but a diffusion of light:
Turtleback returning your gaze,
coyotes' call and response
through the night.

The sunken garden
waits her turn
with secrets you will discover
as you inhabit this place
that repeats its song:
listen … listen to the silence … listen.

Free from Monetary Exchange

Embarrassed or downright angry
at such lack of respect,
the poem says *Don't memorize me
and please don't make children
recite me by heart,
demand they start over
when they forget a word
or lose their place before the end.*

It laughs at restrictions,
rules forcing meaning
into a suit of clothes
two sizes too small
and stitched by imposter hands.

Poetry doesn't want to be a chore
or mashup of AI conceit,
antithesis of human imagination
artificially contrived from bobblehead
to feet planted in sterile soil
or dancing on rocky ground.

It recoils at cliché
and words from other languages
standing in for those
that make it feel at home.

It rejects those ironclad forms
imposed through centuries
of cultures outmoded or dead today,
shuns intentional obscurity,
inflection meant to confuse
or confound.

Its beautiful chaos wants you
to breathe its stanzas in
and exhale astonishment or desire,
longing and fulfillment
you've never known
and cannot find on any map.

The poem wants to touch a place
in the deepest recess of your spirit,
tell you something you don't expect,
light a fire,
ignite your sensibility
and give you what you've never had.

It will always be there
if you trust it to sing
as often as you need to hear
its crooked notes and curious beat,
meet head-on the experience it offers
free from monetary exchange.

Poems Must Say Something

One thing about poems:
they must say something,
were invoked,
created and enriched
to transmit ideas,
experiences,
feelings rescued
from the shadows
of our shame.

Again, and then again,
a poem claims virgin terrain,
fertile land the poet sows
with what she nurtures
in her sleep
or undresses in the light
of each new day.

If the poem mumbles,
ashamed of its words
or embarrassed by conviction
others call strident,
it will disappear
with the ashes of previous fires,
losing itself among the banal
and irrelevant.

If it goes on a rampage
and breaks the bridges
of human connection
it may deafen the reader
as it implodes
in unredeemable pain.

If it chooses those overused words
heard in every soapbox diatribe
or printed on saccharine greeting cards
no one will pay attention
and the poem will be stillborn.

The poem must take risks
and these days risk
may cost a lifetime of peace
and security.
It speaks, dangerous and necessary
to our struggle to survive.

The Prompt

The prompt asks for a word
or several words,
wants me to roll them around
in my mouth,
allow them to collect moss or spit,
bathe themselves until,
bursting between my teeth
and over my lips,
they must escape for air.

Nothing left are the words
I conjure and keep hostage,
forcing them to live
with themselves,
versatile but ominous,
battered by sudden weather events
and rising sea levels,
searching for a safe haven
woven of rain.

Once freed, they are expected
to become a poem
but my words, rebellious
from birth, disappear
before I can tether them
to my lips.

Don't use prompts
or any other trick
to get me started on a poem
or recipe for these dangerous times.
My response will disintegrate
like a papyrus scroll
lost to time.

Protected Speech

This poem appears shy,
curls into a fetal position
and tries to hide
from the books and magazines
that would expose it to contempt.

Its efforts to conform
to syllable count,
submit to the size of the page
and never overstep its margins
seem to have sapped its strength,
keeping it from contention.

It opens its mouth to speak
but only garbled sputtering
fills the air.
No one alive knows its language.

Yet somewhere deep
in its rhythmic pulse
and between its fulsome lines
a rebel lies in wait,
fearless and ready.

Matter's briefest particle,
it is too small to be seen
by the human eye,
too distant to be heard
above the confusion of these times.

But when the moment comes
this poem will appear
ready to take on the world
like the butterfly
that's left its chrysalis behind.

It will tear off its mask,
break with convention
and claim its place
at the center of our story.

It cannot write the end
and neither can you.
Only the fire of resistance
can bring it the relief
of protected speech.

Surf

The surf that hauls my grief ashore
carries numbed faces
of child soldiers
among a tangle of seaweed.

That watery forest
confesses it's testing me:
a devil's advocate
in dangerous times.

I want to fill their eyes
with the tears
all children swallow
when made to perform
beyond their years.

I want to bloody their faces
with dread
or any emotion at all,
tell the marine vegetation
it too has a role to play,
fix this mistake of history.

But my descent into water
makes me complicit
in a story I'd rather rewrite
from the beginning.

We risk too much if we believe
we can ignore these crimes
when winds of change
threaten our anxious readiness.

Ferocious Tenderness

Never, ashamed of its bombast
tries to hide its bulk
behind other words.

Maybe thinks it can hold its own
in a forest that towers
on spindly legs.

Always knows
it has overplayed its hand,
hides behind those
who belittle its name.

X is a bloated letter
pretending to be a word,
vying for a worthy target
as it staggers from sleep.

Words drag meaning behind them
to every momentous gathering,
on every intimate date.

We risk silence
when we subvert them
and they will respond
by leading us down
a dangerous path.

We must nurture those words
placed in our care
with ferocious tenderness
for they will come to our aid
only if they are healthy
and strong enough
to bear their weight.

Dependent on the Calendar's Whim

1.
In this country stretching inland
from its long ribbon of beach,
a woman walking along
an abandoned stretch
looks out at the river
broad enough to be an ocean
through the eyes of her brother
disappeared in 1980.

His disappearance
didn't happen accidentally.
He was taken by a soldier
whose daughter defied her father
by joining the struggle
against such terror and forgetting.

Her memory moves
in different directions now,
depending on the calendar's whim.

A professor remembers
his mother's favorite fruit
was maracuyá.
Not the mother he lost
in the dungeons of that time
but the grandmother
who raised him as her own.

She made a desert from its sweet pulp
and served it in the porcelain dishes
embossed with raised flowers
he uses today when he makes it
for his twins.

This country holds these absences
marking time in its DNA,
splitting or bringing families together.
Children and grandchildren
with empty places at their tables
recall a landscape
painted before they were born.

2.
Back in my distant North
my Acoma friend
feels the Conquest's steel blade
graze his ankle
on the final days of every year.
Its pain carries the memory
of Oñate and his hoards.

Another sees the threat
of flashing lights
each time she gets behind the wheel.
Her car can't forget the cops
who might stop her going 30
and she must prepare her teenage sons
for their brutal script.

In Palestine, Ukraine and Sudan
war sends memory
into an exile
where it may linger for decades.

But we know its seed will sprout
and return one day
in survivor vigilance
and on the tongues of children
who learn early
to chew and spit it out.

I too live with suffocation of memory
surging in my throat
each time I raise my woman's voice.
Like a rain-filled cloud, it hovers
above my head,
a terrible weight
darkening my tiny piece of sky.

Mine is not a nation whose siblings
linger on opposite sides
of warring years
or walk with the ghosts of a story
long exhausted
or hidden from sight.

Dependent on the calendar's whim,
we are all reviving memory now
to prepare for the long forgetting ahead.

The Book Remains

My years trail behind me like a book
I've read again and again,
occasional pages torn
and bearing stains from the rum
I drank before I banished dubious substance
from my skeleton home.

Smoke that once tarred my lungs
is only vague memory now,
a reminder of the day
I decided to leave my body
younger than when
it was entrusted to my care
and age coursed
my veins before birth.

Reaching the end of a trail
four thousand feet
up the mountain from my desert floor
or down where a great river
churns furious rapids
in the deepest canyon of them all,
I wake in ecstasy.

These are memories now,
places my aging body revisits
only in the dreams we keep alive
in stories we offer as gifts
to those who will dig deeper
and climb higher,
writing their own stories
of a beauty that exists
for nothing but itself.

The book remains: hand-printed
in 14-point Bodoni Round,
its supple leather cover
bearing a title that may baffle
the casual reader,
a nameplate with my identity
inscribed in the powerful hand
that continues the work of mine.

The Freedom They Find So Confusing

Because she dresses modestly,
speaks little and has a smile
for everyone,
no one questions
the late-night trips
in her little beige secondhand car.

Those who notice her at all
describe her as mousy,
perfect adjective
when it came to getting
the messages through.

His impeccable writing,
careful cursive praised by teachers
from earliest grades through college,
has other uses now.
No one looks twice
at those ration books
or perfect identity cards.

Their large dinner parties
are the talk of Washington:
pate foie gras
from pigs kept cruelly caged,
filet mignon
so valued in these times,
expensive wines
and a guest list to die for.

Few knoew about the thousands
who did die
on the orders or whim
of the men who linger
at that table,
smoking Gran Habanos
that made it past
the customs official's eye.

She is never invited
to those dinners:
wrong color, age and size.
Her dress
would be wrong,
the conversation
out of her league.

The host and hostess's children
go to a private school
where they're taught to take pride
in the campaign to rid society
of those whose genes
don't enhance the master race
or keep the country great.

Time unfolds
and *never again* struggles
to keep its footing
among endless enticements
to forget.

Today, when the dictator
is only a shameful paragraph
hidden in the history books
to preserve the nation's honor,
those children, elderly now,
still struggle to come to terms
with their feelings
about parents who never had time
for their soccer games
or dance recitals.

Now those children know
they were members
of an invisible army
that risked it all
for the freedom
they find so confusing today.

The Sun Below Our Feet

Where I have been
wants to tell me stories
I know are lies
dressed in clumsy disguises.

My past throws memories
like curve balls
flying by at the speed
of two much good wine.

Even that regal bottle
you held out
as consolation prize,
sure I would fall for its aroma
and breathing coyote glee
when I did.

But I am older now
with less to lose,
have learned to trust
that quiet voice
rising in my throat.

It reminds me the air is purest
at ten thousand feet
where those who reach me
had to labor up the same mountain,
push themselves
beyond the death zone
to witness the sun rising below our feet.

She Began to Speak

She fought off ligatures and time
and began to speak.
It rained and the earth,
parched from indifference and abuse,
held sun-ripened fruit to our lips.

She began to speak. A history
of silence fled our mouths
and settled in that place
where memory tells us who we are.

She began to speak.
The world split open
and all shattered things
came together again.
Young and old
remembered their names.

She began to speak. The wall
of isolation and fear we raised
began to crumble,
its stones returning to the ruins
we tore apart to build this retreat
protected by guns.

Weather on the other side
is predicted mild:
neither fire nor flood
nor winds that can break a heart
but a landscape of hands
joined in desire and industry
welcome us home.

As If Dreaming

Beyond the wishful safety of my home
loud fists knock on vulnerable doors,
shatter some
as they announce that first moment
of deportation: now a common word
and ominously final.

Inside, I cut fresh fruit into bitesize pieces
and make coffee
as I do every morning
while you read about the children starving in Gaza,
the fire that has consumed seventy structures
on Grand Canyon's farthest rim,
yet another Native woman disappeared.

As if dreaming, I follow the headlines
but refuse the stories
I have memorized through decades.
I was the one who could always get away
carrying my secondhand pain
like a bag of sad songs,
their melodies telling the real story.

Will I be the lucky one who escapes but
must juggle this horror streaked with shame
and can only place words
one after another
repeated until the pen drops
from my trembling hand?

The Archive

Tyrants banished him from his country,
robbed her of her citizenship
without asking permission
or giving a reason.
But that wasn't enough.

They followed them to their new homes
in the countries that took them in,
shot them dead
in front of their children
because witnesses must carry the horror.

The tyrant's arms are long, they reach
across borders.
No place is safe from the vengeance
of those who get pleasure
from making others suffer.

And they keep detailed records: how many
delivered to the ovens,
tens of thousands of gold teeth,
the tonnage of shorn hair.
Their archive is their pride.

They don't know the air we breathe
will transform those numbers
into stories of new life, that the sky
reflecting our lamentations
will turn a brighter blue.

Their archive will become a song
heard in all nations,
a poem our children will recite
when memory defeats the lies
and truth can show its face once more.

Where Do We Look

Where do we look for ourselves
when our map is overrun
by this new species
with built-in assault weapons
sulfurous breath
and eyes that accuse?

Some say there's a reservation
where we'll be allowed
to follow our way of life.
Others warn of camps
disguised as seaside resorts
with every amenity.

Those who live in remote regions
try to ignore the black smoke
from ominous chimneys
dotting the horizon,
evidence of a danger
too frightening for words.

Those are precisely the words
begging us to reclaim them
before they disappear
along with the memories
exiting our lives
at the speed of light.

Retrieve the language
our ancestors used
to shape the epic poetry
of a time when tenderness
was enough to make love,
paint a picture
or bake a loaf of bread.

If we find ourselves in a land
where corn grows wild,
honest speech is rewarded
and honest acts are enough,
we will find ourselves
everywhere we look.

Where I Am Going

Where I am going
hides its secrets
beneath piles of words
I cannot hear.

Give it your best shot
I tell myself,
hoping to trick
its code of silence
with my commanding tone.

But my voice cracks
from years of pleading,
strong verbs worn
from trying to shatter
that gloating sneer,
defeat its arrogance.

Despite the cliché
assuring me
everything's going to be
all right,
we don't have
the same finish line
in sight.

One is an armature
of bombast
standing at attention
as its tired troops
march by.

The other,
as mysterious
as summer rain,
descends in temperatures
too erratic for nurture.

Only the land can speak
our name
with a single voice,
bring us together
in a space we must learn
to navigate with sure feet.

Where I am going
is behind me now.
I look back and wave
as I take my leave,
waiting for the last breath
that, erasing my pulse,
will bequeath my memory
to those who pick up the scent.

Margaret Randall (b. New York, 1936) is a poet, essayist, oral historian, translator, photographer, and social activist. She is the author of more than two hundred books. She lived in Latin America for twenty-three years (in Mexico, Cuba, and Nicaragua). From 1962 to 1969, she and Mexican poet Sergio Mondragón co-edited *El Corno Emplumado / The Plumed Horn*, a bilingual literary quarterly that published some of the best new literature and art of the sixties.

When she came home in 1984, the government ordered her deported because it found some of her writing to be "against the good order and happiness of the United States." With the support of many writers and others, she won her case and her citizenship was restored in 1989.

Randall's recent titles include poetry, essays, and other creative nonfiction. These include her 2020 memoir *I Never Left Home: Poet, Feminist, Revolutionary* (Duke University Press) and two volumes of selected poems called *Time's Language* (Wings Press).

Her most recent projects include two books based on her correspondence with people she calls "outriders," creatives who have faced serious obstacles but have pushed through them to make and do. *Letters from the Edge* and *More Letters from the Edge* have been published by New Village Press. She has also recently published a book of essays, *Pages Lost and New*, from Casa Urraca Press, following up the previous collections *Last Words* and *Thinking About Thinking*.

Many of Randall's titles have appeared in Spanish translation from Siglo XXI, Alforja, Ediciones de Medianoche, and Heredad in Mexico; Casa de las Américas, Ediciones Matanzas, and Vigía in Cuba; Abisinia and Tinta Limón in Argentina, Rumbo in Uruguay, and independent publishers in Nicaragua, Brazil, Ecuador, Peru, Colombia, Venezuela, Spain, Holland, Japan, Turkey, and India.

Randall also translates from the Spanish. She has produced English-language poetry collections by Roberto Fernández Retamar, Roque Dalton, Otto-René Castillo, Carlos María Gutiérrez, Daisy Zamora, Kelly Martínez, Israel Domínguez, Alfredo Zaldívar, Laura Ruíz, Chely Lima, Rita Valdivia, Reynaldo García Blanco, Yanira Marimón, and Gaudencio Rodríguez Santana, among others; novels by Freddy Prestol Castillo, Juan Antonio Hernández, and Tomás Modesto Galán; memoirs by Gregory Randall, Lurgio Gavilán Sánchez, and Stefano Varese; and anthologies of Cuban poetry and short stories, Ecuadorean poetry, U.S. poets for Mexico, and Beat Poets in Spanish. She has read her own work and delivered keynote addresses in hundreds of venues throughout the United States, Latin America, and other countries.

Two of Randall's photographs are in the Capitol Art Collection in Santa Fe. In 1960 Randall was a recipient of a Carnegie Fund for Writers Aid Grant and a grant from the American Academy of Arts and Letters revolving fund for writers in need. In 1989 she was a co-winner of the Mencken Award, and in 1990 she received a Lillian Hellman and Dashiell Hammett grant for writers victimized by political repression. The Barbara Deming Money for Women Award was given to her in 1997, and in 2004 she received the PEN New Mexico Dorothy Doyle Lifetime Achievement Award for Writing and Human Rights Activism. Randall received the 2017 Medalla al Mérito Literario, awarded by Literatura en el Bravo in Ciudad Juárez, Mexico. In 2018 she was awarded the Poet of Two Hemispheres prize by Poesía en Paralelo Cero in Quito, Ecuador. In 2019 she was awarded an honorary doctorate of letters from the University of New Mexico, and in 2020 she received the George Garrett Award from the Association of Writers & Writing Programs (AWP) and the Paulo Freire Award from Chapman University. She received the City of Albuquerque's Creative Bravo Award in 2022.

Randall lives in Albuquerque with her partner (now wife) of more than thirty-nine years, the painter Barbara Byers, and travels extensively to read, lecture, and teach.

Casa Urraca Press

Casa Urraca Press publishes creative nonfiction, poetry, fiction, and other works by authors we believe in. New Mexico and the U.S. Southwest are rich in creative and literary talent, and the rest of the world deserves to experience our perspectives. So we champion books that belong in the conversation—books with the power, compassion, and variety to bring very different people closer together.

We were proudly founded in the high desert somewhere near Abiquiú, New Mexico. Visit us at casaurracapress.com to read more from our authors, browse all editions of our books, and register for writing workshops and retreats.

www.ingramcontent.com/pod-product-compliance
Lightning Source LLC
LaVergne TN
LVHW040057080526
838202LV00045B/3680